ST JOHN THE EVANGELIST & ST VERENA
Coptic Orthodox Church
Armadale - Victoria

PASSION WEEK FOR KIDS

His Holiness Pope Tawadros II
The 118th Pope of Alexandria and Patriarch of
the See of Saint Mark

Dear Blessed Congregation of St. John and St. Verena Coptic Orthodox Church.

The blessed fathers want to express their immense gratitude to the servants and all who participated with this book on Passion Week for our children, which encompasses puzzles, drawings, multimedia and visual aids to help to attract and benefit our blessed children.

As Isaiah 54:13 writes, "All your children shall be taught by the Lord, and great shall be the peace of your children." Furthermore, the Psalmist writes in Psalm 127:3 "Behold, children are a gift from the Lord, they are a reward from him."

Considering the above verses, children are a precious gift from God, and the onus is on the church to teach. Hence, this resource confirms our enduring commitment to realise and nourish our children in their development and growth in faith. So that God grants them the gift of peace in their lives building on this resource and potential future developments.

May God bless you all who tired in producing this resource.

Fathers of St. John and St. Verena Church.

CONTENTS

Holy Week

—— HOLIEST WEEK OF THE YEAR ——

Also known as the "Pascha (aka Passover) Feast."

Runs for six days - from Palm Sunday to Joyous Saturday.

It is a special week added to the Great Lent to focus the Church on the sufferings of the Lord

Some Interesting Things To Look Out For!

There is **NO** raising of incense from Monday until Wednesday.

None of the sacraments are performed (except for confession).

The first sacrament you will see is the Divine Liturgy celebrated on Covenant Thursday.

This is a symbol of the Passover lamb **(Christ),** which was kept for four days before it was sacrificed.

The Church prepares the congregation for the lack of these sacraments by having general services called Pascha.

PALM SUNDAY

Blessed is He Who Comes in the Name of the Lord

Luke 19:38

Palm Sunday

Summary of Palm Sunday

Known as <u>"Hosanna Sunday"</u> or <u>"Palm Sunday"</u>.
It is the seventh Sunday in the Great Lent

We call it "Palm" Sunday because the crowds were waving palm andolive branches to welcome Jesus to Jerusalem.

When the crowds saw Jesus riding into Jerusalem, they started chanting at the top of their voices 'Hosanna!' which is the Greek word for 'Save Us!'

The Church is decorated with Palm Branches to remind us of what thepeople in Jerusalem did when they saw Jesus enter the city.

Everyone has a great time making crosses and other designs from palms to wave during mass.

SCAN ME

Rites of Palm Sunday

Palm Sunday in the Coptic Orthodox Churchhas a special rite which means there are special actions and words that need to be said and performed during the service.

<u>All Hymns during this service are said in a joyful Palm Sunday tune</u>

During the offering of the morning incense, Abouna and the Deacons have a processionaround the Church carrying the Holy cross, candles, palm and olive branches, flowers, incense, and the icon of the entry of Our Lord into Jerusalem.

- Twelve readings from the Holy Gospel are read at different locations around the church.
- Four Gospels are read during the Liturgy:

  o Matthew 21: 1-17

  o Mark 11:1-10

  o Luke 19:28-46

  o John 12:12-19

- Abouna says the prayer of the Holy Gospel twice, one before the first Gospel and the second one before the fourth Gospel.
- The Holy Liturgy then continues as usual until communion where we sing a special Palm Sunday hymn

DOXOLOGY

DID YOU KNOW?
Doxology means a confirmation of glory to the holy trinity. We pray the Doxology in Vespers andmatins of Palm Sunday.

Blow the trumpet at the new moon: with the sound of the trumpet: on your festive day: for it is an order from God.

He who sits upon the Cherubim: rode on a donkey: and entered into Jerusalem: what is this great humility.

According to what David said: in the psalms: Blessed is He who comes inthe name of the Lord of hosts.

Again he said: Out of the mouths of the babes: and nursing infants: You have perfected praise.

Then He completed the saying: of David the spirit-bearer: who likewise said: out of the mouths of the little children.

They praise Him watchfully: saying, This is Immanuel: hosanna in the highest: this is the King of Israel.

Bring to the Lord, O sons of God: bring to the Lord glory and honor: rejoice in our God: with doxologies of blessing.

Praise is due to You, O God: in Zion and Jerusalem: they send to You: prayers unto the ages.

Hosanna in the highest: this is the King of Israel: blessed is He, who comes in the name: of the Lord of hosts.

We praise Him and glorify Him: and exalt Him above all: as the Good One and Lover of Mankind: have mercy on us according to Your great mercy.

Palm Sunday

EVLOGIMENOS

Blessed is He who comes in the Name of the Lord; again, in the Name of the Lord.

Hosanna to the Son of David; again, to the Son of David.

Hosanna in the highest; again, in the highest.

Hosanna to the King of Israel; again, to the King of Israel.

Let us chant saying: Alleluia, Alleluia, Alleluia.

Glory be to our God; again, glory be to our God.

DID YOU KNOW?
Evlogimenos is one of the most popular hymns of our church. We chant this hymn on Palm Sunday during Vespers, Matins, Liturgy of the Word and the Distribution of the Holy Mysteries. We also chant it during the entrance of the Pope, Metropolitan or Bishop into the church.

HOSANNA IN THE HIGHEST

Hosanna in the highest, this is the King of Israel, Blessed is He who comes in the name of the Lord of Hosts.	Oasanna khen ne-etchosi, fai ep-ooro em-Pysraeel, efesmaroaoot enge fe-ethneeoo, ken efran emepchois ente nigom.	Ⲱⲥⲁⲛⲛⲁ ϧⲉⲛ ⲛⲏⲉⲧϭⲟⲥⲓ: ⲫⲁⲓ ⲡⲉ Ⲡⲟⲩⲣⲟ ⲙ̀Ⲡⲓⲥⲣⲁⲏⲗ: ϥ̀ⲥⲙⲁⲣⲱⲟⲩⲧ ⲛ̀ⲭⲉ Ⲫⲏⲉⲑⲛⲏⲟⲩ: ϧⲉⲛ ⲫⲣⲁⲛ ⲙ̀Ⲡϭⲟⲓⲥ ⲛ̀ⲧⲉ ⲛⲓϫⲟⲙ.

Palm Sunday

PSALM RESPONSE - VESPERS

Alleluia, Alleluia. Jesus Christ, the Son of God, entered into Jerusalem. Alleluia, Alleluia.

GOSPEL RESPONSE - VESPERS

Hail to Lazarus, whom He raised, after four days, raise my heart O my Lord Jesus, that was killed by the evil one.

Blessed be the Father, and the Son, and the Holy Spirit. The Perfect Trinity, we worship Him and glorify Him.

CONCLUDING CANON

Amen. Alleluia.

Glory to the Father and to the Son and to the Holy Spirit. Now and ever and unto the ages of the ages. Amen.

We proclaim and say, O our Lord Jesus Christ. The Son of God entered into Jerusalem. Save us and have mercy on us.

Lord have mercy, Lord have mercy, Lord bless us. Amen, Bless me, Bless me. Lo, the repentance. Forgive me, Say the blessing.

Palm Sunday

HOSANNA TO THE KING OF KINGS

GOSPEL RESPONSES - LITURGY

St. Matthew's Gospel

Hosanna in the highest, this is the King of Israel, blessedis He who comes in the name, of the lord of hosts.

St. Mark's Gospel

He who sits upon the cherubim, today appeared in Jerusalem, riding on a colt with great glory, surrounded by ranks of angels.

St. Luke's Gospel

On the road they spread garments, and from the trees they cut branches, while proclaiming with hymns, Hosanna to the Son of David.

St. John's Gospel

Today the sayings are fulfilled, from the prophecies and proverbs, as Zachariah prophesised and said, a prophecy about Jesus Christ.

PSALM 150

Alleluia, Alleluia, Alleluia, Alleluia.
Jesus Christ, the Son of God, entered into Jerusalem.

Palm Sunday

Palm Sunday

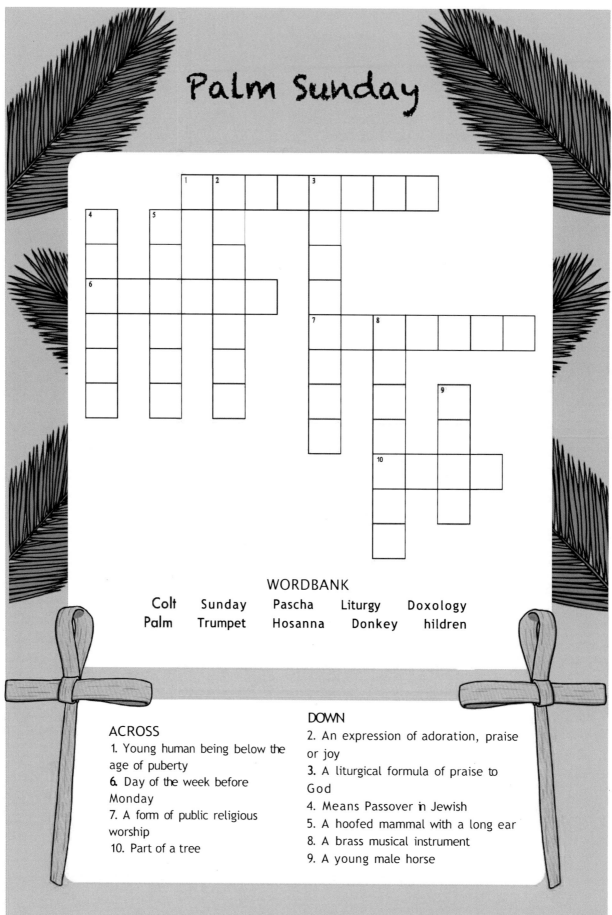

WORDBANK

Colt	Sunday	Pascha	Liturgy	Doxology
Palm	Trumpet	Hosanna	Donkey	hildren

ACROSS
1. Young human being below the age of puberty
6. Day of the week before Monday
7. A form of public religious worship
10. Part of a tree

DOWN
2. An expression of adoration, praise or joy
3. A liturgical formula of praise to God
4. Means Passover in Jewish
5. A hoofed mammal with a long ear
8. A brass musical instrument
9. A young male horse

General Funeral Prayer

Summary of General Funeral Prayer

- A General Funeral Prayer is said right after the Palm Sunday Liturgy.
- We Pray this as no incense can be raised for people who pass away during Holy Week.
- A bowl of water is placed at the front of the Church.
- Abouna prays a number of special prayers on the water.
- <u>The prayers are said in a sad mournful tune.</u>
- At the end of the prayers Abouna blesses the congregation with the water.

Rites of General Funeral Prayer

- After the conclusion of the Liturgy, Abouna closes the veil of the Sanctuary (Altar) and Prayers are said in the following order:
    - Prophecies
    - Thanksgiving prayer
    - Introduction of the Pauline epistle in a special mournful tune
    - Pauline epistle
    - *Trisagion* - Holy God, Holy Mighty, Holy Immortal who was crucified for our sake three times
    - Psalm and Gospel in a sad mournful tune
    - Three long Litanies - Peace, Fathers and Congregation
    - The Creed
    - Litany of the departed
    - The Lord's Prayer (Our Father)
    - Three absolutions.
    - Raising the cross, Abouna chants *Efnoti nai nan* followed by 12 *Kyrie eleison*
    - *Eporo* in the Paschal tune
    - Concluding canon (Amen Allelujia...)
    - Abouna's blessing

General Funeral Prayer

CONCLUDING HYMN

Lord have mercy (*each side 3 times for a total of 12 times*)	Kyrie eleson	Ⲕⲩⲣⲓⲉ̀ ⲉ̀ⲗⲉⲏⲥⲟⲛ
O King of peace, grant us Your peace, establish for us Your peace, and forgive us our sins.	Epouro enteti hirini moynan entek hirini semni nan entek hirini kanen novi nan evol.	Ⲡⲟⲩⲣⲟ ⲛ̀ⲧⲉ ϯ϶ⲓⲣⲏⲛⲏ: ⲙⲟⲓ ⲛⲁⲛ ⲛ̀ⲧⲉⲕϩⲓⲣⲏⲛⲏ: ⲥⲉⲙⲛⲓ ⲛⲁⲛ ⲛ̀ⲧⲉⲕϩⲓⲣⲏⲛⲏ: ⲭⲁ ⲛⲉⲛⲛⲟⲃⲓ ⲛⲁⲛ ⲉ̀ⲃⲟⲗ.
Lord have mercy (x6)	Kyrie eleson	Ⲕⲩⲣⲓⲉ̀ ⲉ̀ⲗⲉⲏⲥⲟⲛ
Disperse the enemies, of the Church, and fortify her, that she may not be shaken forever.	Gorh evol enni gaji enteti ekekleseya ari soft eros enneskem sha-eneh.	Ⲭⲱⲣ ⲉⲃⲟⲗ ⲛ̀ⲛⲓⲭⲁϫⲓ: ⲛ̀ⲧⲉ ϯⲉⲕⲕⲗⲏⲥⲓⲁ̀: ⲁⲣⲓⲥⲟⲃⲧ ⲉⲣⲟⲥ: ⲛ̀ⲛⲉⲥⲕⲓⲙ ϣⲁ ⲉ̀ⲛⲉϩ.
Lord have mercy (x6)	Kyrie eleson	Ⲕⲩⲣⲓⲉ̀ ⲉ̀ⲗⲉⲏⲥⲟⲛ
Immanuel our God, is now in our midst, with the glory of His Father, and the Holy Spirit.	Emmanoeel Pennoti khen tenmeeti tino khen ep-oo ente Peviot nem Pi-epnevma Ethowab.	Ⲉⲙⲙⲁⲛⲟⲩⲏⲗ ⲡⲉⲛⲛⲟⲩϯ: ϧⲉⲛ ⲧⲉⲛⲙⲏϯ ϯⲛⲟⲩ: ϧⲉⲛ ⲡ̀ⲱ̀ⲟⲩ ⲛ̀ⲧⲉ ⲡⲉϥⲓⲱⲧ: ⲛⲉⲙ ⲡⲓⲡⲛⲁ ⲉⲑⲟⲩⲁⲃ.
Lord have mercy (x6)	Kyrie eleson	Ⲕⲩⲣⲓⲉ̀ ⲉ̀ⲗⲉⲏⲥⲟⲛ
May He bless us all, and purify our hearts, and heal the sicknesses of our souls and bodies.	Entefesmo eron tiren entef tovo ennen heet entev talet sho enni sho ni ente nen epsishi nem nen soma.	Ⲛ̀ⲧⲉϥⲥ̀ⲙⲟⲩ ⲉⲣⲟⲛ ⲧⲏⲣⲉⲛ: ⲛ̀ⲧⲉϥⲧⲟⲃⲟ ⲛ̀ⲛⲉⲛϩⲏⲧ: ⲛ̀ⲧⲉϥⲧⲁⲗϬⲟ ⲛ̀ⲛⲓϣⲱⲛⲓ: ⲛ̀ⲧⲉ ⲛⲉⲛⲯⲩⲭⲏ ⲛⲉⲙ ⲛⲉⲛⲥⲱⲙⲁ.
Lord have mercy (x6)	Kyrie eleson	Ⲕⲩⲣⲓⲉ̀ ⲉ̀ⲗⲉⲏⲥⲟⲛ
We worship You O Christ, with Your T Father, and the Holy Spirit, for you were crucified and save us.	Ten oa-osht emmok o Pi-ekhrestos nem Pekyot en aghathos nem Pi-epnevma ethowab je av ashk aksoti emmon.	Ⲧⲉⲛⲟⲩⲱϣⲧ ⲙ̀ⲙⲟⲕ ⲱ̀ Ⲡⲭ̅ⲥ̅: ⲛⲉⲙ ⲡⲉⲕⲓⲱⲧ ⲛ̀ⲁ̀ⲅⲁⲑⲟⲥ: ⲛⲉⲙ ⲡⲓⲡⲛⲁ ⲉⲑⲟⲩⲁⲃ ⲭⲉ ⲁⲩⲁϣⲕ ⲁⲕⲥⲱϯ ⲙ̀ⲙⲟⲛ.

General Funeral Prayer

CONCLUDING CANON

Amen. Alleluia.

Glory to the Father and to the Son and to the Holy Spirit.

Now and ever and unto the ages of the ages. Amen.

We proclaim and say, O our Lord Jesus Christ, who was crucified on thecross, trampled Satan under our feet.

Save us and have mercy on us.

Lord have mercy, Lord have mercy, Lord bless us Amen, Bless me, Blessme. Lo, the repentance. Forgive me, Say the blessing.

PASSION
WEEK

"He was silent and quietly endured everything...to teach us all about meekness and longsuffering. let us now imitate him "
St. John Chrysostom

PASSION WEEK SUMMARY

The last week of Lent is called Passion Week or Holy Week

All the prayers and readings help us remember and understand the events that led up to the crucifixion and the resurrection of our Lord Jesus Christ.

> **ACTIVITY**
> Memorise the theme of each Pascha summarised on the next page

PASSION WEEK RITES

Each day of Passion Week is divided into _evening_ and _morning_ prayers called Pascha (Passover)

Each Pascha is divided into 1st, 3rd, 6th, 9th and 11th Hour prayers (12th Hour is added on Great Friday)

Pascha prayers are prayed **OUTSIDE** the Sanctuary (Altar) following Christ who was crucified outside of Jerusalem.

The Church is decorated in **black** to show our sadness. We are sad because we remember our sins and what happened to Christ this week because of them.

- We are all encouraged to read each Gospel from start to finish:
  - The Gospel according to St. Matthew on Tuesday
  - The Gospel according to St. Mark on Wednesday
  - The Gospel according to St. Luke on Thursday
  - The Gospel according to St. John on Sunday

From Wednesday Eve until the end of Saturday, we don't greet each other by kissing, as a reminder of how Judas betrayed Jesus with a kiss

<u>The Paschal Services follow this order:</u>

Prophecies ➔ The Paschal Praise (Thok Te Ti Gom) x 12 Times ➔ Psalm and Gospel (Mournful Tune) ➔ Commentaries ➔ Litanies ➔ Conclusion and Blessing

Passion Week Summary

Palm Sunday
Jesus rides a donkey into Jerusalem.

Monday
Jesus curses the fig tree that had leaves but no fruit.

Monday / Tuesday Eve (Monday Night)
Jesus removes all the buyers and sellers from the temple because the temple is a Holy place for prayer.

Tuesday
Parables and prophesies of Christ's second coming reminding us to keep watch and fill our lamps.

Second Coming

Wednesday Eve (Tuesday Night)
We are reminded of to keep watch. Parable of the 5 Wise virgins.

Wednesday
Mary of Bethany shows her love to Christ by anointing His feet with oil and perfume.

Thursday Eve (Wednesday Night)
Judas strats the plan to betray Jesus by accepting 30 pieces of Silver from the Jews.

Covenant Thursday
(Washing of the feet) Jesus prepares the last supper and washes the feet of the disciples

Great Friday Eve (Thursday Night)
Jesus prayes in the Garden of Gethsemane Judas betrays Jesus with a kisss, Jesus is arrested.

Great Friday
The Chief Priests condemn Jesus and take Him to be crucified and buried. Jesus becomes the perfect sacrifice for us.

Joyous Saturday
Jesus in the tomb

Monday

Summary of Monday

On Monday while Christ was on the way to Bethany, he cursed a fig tree because it had lots of leaves but no fruit. Normally fig trees have lots of fruit! This tree represented the Jewish people, who knew what they had to do through all the laws and rituals, yet they had not followed them and done good works. On the other hand, the tree can also represent us today!

We can look from the outside like good Christians, but not behave like Christ.

Jesus also enters the temple on the Monday and casts out all the people who were buying and selling because they had turned the holy temple into a marketplace.

This upset Jesus as His House is a place for Prayer.

SCAN ME

Monday

Follow Jesus' journey on Monday from Bethany to the temple!!

START

At Bethany, Jesus had many friends. He visited often with Mary and Martha, and their brother, Lazarus.

There He entered the temple and cast out the moneychangers and overthrew the tables of the men selling doves.

START

PASCHA PRAISE (THOK TE TI GOM)

To you is the Power, the Glory the Blessing, the Majesty forever amen, Emmanuel Our God and Our King.	Thok te ti-gom, nem pi-o-oo nem pi-esmo, nem pi-amhahee sha eneh amen, Emmano-eel pen-nouti pen-oroo.	Ⲑⲱⲕ ⲧⲉ ϯϫⲟⲙ ⲛⲉⲙ ⲡⲓⲱⲟⲩ ⲛⲉⲙ ⲡⲓⲥⲙⲟⲩ ⲛⲉⲙ Ⲡⲓⲁⲙⲁϩⲓ ϣⲁ ⲉⲛⲉϩ ⲁⲙⲏⲛ: Ⲉⲙⲙⲁⲛⲟⲩⲏⲗ ⲡⲉⲛⲛⲟⲩϯ ⲡⲉⲛⲟⲩⲣⲟ.
To you is the Power, the Glory the Blessing, the Majesty forever amen, My Lord Jesus Christ.	Thok te ti-gom, nem pi-o-oo nem pi-esmo, nem pi-amhahee sha eneh amen, pa-Shois Esos Piekh-restos.	Ⲑⲱⲕ ⲧⲉ ϯϫⲟⲙ ⲛⲉⲙ ⲡⲓⲱⲟⲩ ⲛⲉⲙ ⲡⲓⲥⲙⲟⲩ ⲛⲉⲙ Ⲡⲓⲁⲙⲁϩⲓ ϣⲁ ⲉⲛⲉϩ ⲁⲙⲏⲛ: Ⲡⲁⲟ̅ⲥ̅ Ⲓ̅ⲏ̅ⲥ̅ Ⲡ̅ⲭ̅ⲥ̅.
To you is the Power, the Glory the Blessing, the Majesty forever Amen.	Thok te ti-gom, nem pi-o-oo nem pi-esmo, nem pi-amhahee sha eneh amen.	Ⲑⲱⲕ ⲧⲉ ϯϫⲟⲙ ⲛⲉⲙ ⲡⲓⲱⲟⲩ ⲛⲉⲙ ⲡⲓⲥⲙⲟⲩ ⲛⲉⲙ Ⲡⲓⲁⲙⲁϩⲓ ϣⲁ ⲉⲛⲉϩ ⲁⲙⲏⲛ.

DID YOU KNOW?
Thok Te Ti Gom is a praise sung by the angels in Heaven!
(Revelations, 5:12-13 and 7:12)

KE EPERTO

We beseech our Lord and God, that we may be worthy to hear the Holy Gospel. In wisdom, let us listen to the Holy Gospel.	Ke Eipertoo Kataxioatheene eeemas, tees akro aseoas too agioo evangelioo, kyrion ke to theon eemoan. Eyketevsoamen sofia orthi akoosoamen too agio evanelio.	Ⲕⲉ ⲩ̀ⲡⲉⲣⲧⲟⲩ ⲕⲁⲧⲁⲍⲓⲱⲑⲏⲛⲉ ⲏ̀ⲙⲁⲥ: ⲧⲏⲥ ⲁⲕⲣⲟ ⲁ̀ⲥⲉⲱ̀ⲥ ⲧⲟⲩ ⲁ̀ⲅⲓⲟⲩ ⲉⲩⲁ̀ⲅⲅⲉⲗⲓⲟⲩ: ⲕⲩⲣⲓⲟⲛ ⲕⲉ ⲧⲟⲛ ⲑⲉⲟⲛ ⲏ̀ⲙⲱⲛ: ⲓ̀ⲕⲉⲧⲉⲩⲥⲱⲙⲉⲛ ⲥⲟⲫⲓⲁ ⲟⲣⲑⲓ ⲁ̀ⲕⲟⲩⲥⲱⲙⲉⲛ ⲧⲟⲩ ⲁ̀ⲅⲓⲟⲩ ⲉⲩⲁ̀ⲅⲅⲉⲗⲓⲟⲩ.

Monday

PSALM – 6TH HOUR OF MONDAY DAY

From the Psalms of our father David the Prophet and King. May his blessings be with us. Amen.

Psalm 121: 4
There the tribes went up, the tribes of the Lord, a testimony to Israel.
To give thanks to the name of the Lord.
Alleluia.

GOSPEL – 6TH HOUR OF MONDAY DAY

*O God have mercy and compassion upon us and make us worthy to hear the Holy Gospel. A reading according
to St. John. May his blessings be with us all. Amen.*

John 2: 13-17

And Jesus went up to Jerusalem. And He found in the temple those who sold oxen and sheep and doves, and the money changers doing business. When he had made a whip of cords, He drove them all out of the temple, with the sheep and the oxen, and poured out the changers' money and overturned the tables. And He said to those who sold doves, "Take these things away! Do not make My Father's house a house of merchandise!" Then His disciples remembered that it was written, "Zeal for your house has eaten Me up."

Bow down before the Holy Gospel.
Glory be to God forever.

EXPOSITION

Christ Our Saviour has come and has borne suffering that through His Passion He may save us.
Let us Glorify Him and exalt His Name, for He has done us mercy, according to His great mercy.

EXPOSITION INTRODUCTION

Priest: In the name of the Trinity
People: One in Essence,
Priest: The Father and the Son,
People: And the Holy Spirit

<u>During the Daytime hours of Pascha the following is said:</u>

Priest: O True Light
People: Who enlightens,
Priest: Every man,
People: Who comes into the world.

<u>During the Night time hours of Pascha the following is said:</u>

Priest: Hail to you, Mary
People: The fair dove
Priest: Who has born unto us
People: God the Logos

EXPOSITION CONCLUSION

Priest: Christ our Saviour
People: Has come and has borne suffering
Priest: That through His Passion
People: He may save us.
Priest: Let us glorify Him
People: And exalt His name
Priest: For He has done us mercy
People: According to His great mercy.

Tuesday

Summary of Tuesday

Tuesday is known as the day of <u>parables and prophesies.</u> Two of the most well-known Parable were said on this day – The Talents and The Ten Virgins.

Jesus used Parables as a way to answer questions from his disciples andto answer the Pharisees and Sadducees (Jews), who had tried to trap Him. By trap him we mean they were trying to catch Him saying something wrong or against the Jewish Law.

The major theme of Tuesday is around the second coming of Jesus Christand the necessity to remain watchful and to keep our lamps lit, just like the 5 wise virgins.

SCAN ME

<u>Decode the Message!</u>

A	B	C	D	E	F	G	H	I	J	K	L	M	N	O	P	Q	R	S	T	U	V	W	X	Y	Z
			8					12							19		2	6							

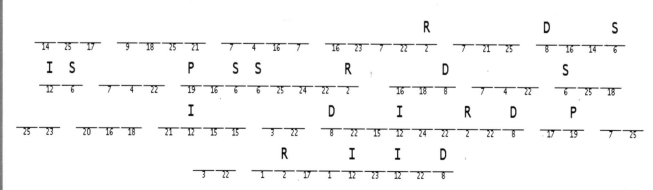

PASCHA PRAISE (THOK TE TI GOM)

To you is the Power, the Glory the Blessing, the Majesty forever amen, Emmanuel Our God and Our King.	Thok te ti-gom, nem pi-o-oo nem pi-esmo, nem pi-amhahee sha eneh amen, Emmano-eel pen-nouti pen-oroo.	Ⲑⲱⲕ ⲧⲉ ϯϫⲟⲙ ⲛⲉⲙ ⲡⲓⲱⲟⲩ ⲛⲉⲙ ⲡⲓⲥⲙⲟⲩ ⲛⲉⲙ Ⲡⲓⲁⲙⲁϩⲓ ϣⲁ ⲉⲛⲉϩ ⲁⲙⲏⲛ: Ⲉⲙⲙⲁⲛⲟⲩⲏⲗ ⲡⲉⲛⲛⲟⲩϯ ⲡⲉⲛⲟⲩⲣⲟ.
To you is the Power, the Glory the Blessing, the Majesty forever amen, My Lord Jesus Christ. My Good Saviour.	Thok te ti-gom, nem pi-o-oo nem pi-esmo, nem pi-amhahee sha eneh amen, pa-Shois Esos Piekh-restos. Pasoteer en-aghathos.	Ⲑⲱⲕ ⲧⲉ ϯϫⲟⲙ ⲛⲉⲙ ⲡⲓⲱⲟⲩ ⲛⲉⲙ ⲡⲓⲥⲙⲟⲩ ⲛⲉⲙ Ⲡⲓⲁⲙⲁϩⲓ ϣⲁ ⲉⲛⲉϩ ⲁⲙⲏⲛ: Ⲡⲁⲟ̅ⲥ̅ Ⲓⲏ̅ⲥ̅ Ⲡⲭ̅ⲥ̅: ⲡⲁⲥⲱⲧⲉⲣ ⲛ̀ⲁⲅⲁⲑⲟⲥ:
To you is the Power, the Glory the Blessing, the Majesty forever amen.	Thok te ti-gom, nem pi-o-oo nem pi-esmo, nem pi-amhahee sha eneh amen.	Ⲑⲱⲕ ⲧⲉ ϯϫⲟⲙ ⲛⲉⲙ ⲡⲓⲱⲟⲩ ⲛⲉⲙ ⲡⲓⲥⲙⲟⲩ ⲛⲉⲙ Ⲡⲓⲁⲙⲁϩⲓ ϣⲁ ⲉⲛⲉϩ ⲁⲙⲏⲛ.

DID YOU KNOW?

On the 11th hour prayers of Tuesday, the phrase "my Good Saviour" is added because in this hour's Gospel reading the Lord Jesus has revealed when he would be crucified.

KE EPERTO

See Page. 25 for QR Code

Tuesday

PSALM – 3ʳᴰ HOUR OF TUESDAY DAY

From the Psalms of our father David the Prophet and King. May his blessings be with us. Amen.

Psalm 119: 154-155

Plead my cause and redeem me; give me life because of your word.

Salvation is far from sinners, for they have not searched Your ordinances.

Alleluia.

GOSPEL – 3ʳᴰ HOUR OF TUESDAY DAY

O God have mercy and compassion upon us and make us worthy to hear to the Holy Gospel. A reading according to St. Matthew. May his blessings be with us all. Amen.

Matthew 23: 37- 24:2

TRY THIS AT HOME

"O Jerusalem, Jerusalem the one who kill the prophets and stones those who are sent to her! How often I wanted to gather your children together, as a hen gathers her chicks under her wings but you were not willing! See! Your house is left to you desolate; for I say to you, you shall see Me no more till you say, 'Blessed is He who comes in the name of the Lord!'"

Then Jesus went out and departed from the temple, and His disciples came up to show Him the buildings of the temple. And Jesus said to them, "Do you not see all these things? Assuredly I say to you, not one stone shall be left here upon another, that shall not be thrown down."

Bow down before the Holy Gospel.
Glory be to God forever.

EXPOSITION

See Page. 26-27 for QR Code

Wednesday

Wednesday is a day of two completely opposite events!

Amazing love shown by Mary	Betrayal of Judas

Mary anoints the feet of Jesus with expensive precious oil.

This oil could have bought foodfor a family for a WHOLE YEAR!!

Mary loved Jesus so much, thatshe didn't care how much it would cost.

Judas spent so much time with Jesus, as one of his disciples, and saw all his works and miracles.

In the end he betrayed Jesus and sold Him to the Jews and chief priests for only 30 pieces of silver.

SCAN ME

Wednesday

```
B   A   T   H   I   R   T   Y   D   B   U   L
E   T   N   J   E   S   L   R   U   S   A   S
T   S   A   O   I   A   A   D   L   Y   A   E
H   T   H   E   I   N   R   E   A   C   A   L
A   O   N   R   E   N   V   R   R   E   S   H
N   E   U   K   H   O   T   I   A   S   K   E
Y   B   I   P   L   E   F   I   T   T   H   I
S   P   F   O   B   I   D   E   N   A   R   I
S   R   T   H   C   E   D   A   Y   G   O   F
T   H   R   E   E   H   U   N   D   R   E   D
M   Y   B   H   S   A   W   U   R   I   A   L
L   U   F   H   T   I   A   F   O   D   V   P
```

WORDBANK

Anointing Burial Love Thirty Bethany Denari
Sacrifice Three Hundred Betrayal Faithful Spikenard Wash

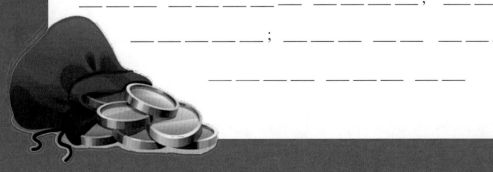

Secret Message!!

Find all the word in the wordsearch and then use the remaining letters to find the secret message.

____ _____ _____, " ___ ____

_____ ; ____ __ ____

____ ___ __

KE EPERTO

See Page. 25 for QR Code

PSALM – 9TH HOUR OF WEDNESDAY DAY

From the Psalms of our father David the Prophet and King. May his blessings be with us. Amen.

Psalm 40: 6-8
My enemies speak evil things against me.

Against me they devise evils for me. And if he comes to see us, He speaks in vain; his heart gathered lawlessness to itself.

Alleluia.

GOSPEL – 9TH HOUR OF WEDNESDAY DAY

O God have mercy and compassion upon us and make us worthy to hear the Holy Gospel. A reading according to St. John. May his blessings be with us all.
Amen.

Matthew 26: 3-16

Then the chief priests, the scribes, and the elders of the people assembled at the palace of the high priest, who was called Caiaphas, and plotted to take Jesus by trickery and kill him. But they said, "Not during the feast, lest there be an uproar among the people." And when Jesus was in Bethany at the house of Simon the leper, a woman came to Him having an alabaster flask of very costly fragrant oil, and she poured it on His head as He sat at the table. But when His disciples saw it, they were indignant saying, "Why this waste? For this fragrant oil might have been sold for much and given to the poor." But when Jesus was aware of it, He said to them, "Why do you trouble the woman? For she has done a good work for Me. For you have the poor with you always, but Me you do not have always. For in pouring this fragrant oil on my body, she did it for my burial, Assuredly I say to you wherever this gospel is preached in the whole world, what this woman has done will also be told as a memorial to her."

TRY THIS AT HOME

34

Wednesday

GOSPEL – 9TH HOUR OF WEDNESDAY DAY

Then one of the twelve, Judas called Iscariot, went to the chief priests and said, "What are you willing to give me if I deliver Him to you?" And they counted out to him thirty pieces of silver. So from that time he sought opportunity to betray him.

Bow down before the Holy Gospel.
Glory be to God forever.

EXPOSITION

See Page. 26-27 for QR Code

COVENANT THURSDAY

"We thank God that when we were outside the city, carrying the shame of sin, the Lord opened the door of the Holy of Holies to us. He opens to us His holy altar and gives us His Holy Body and Holy Blood. It is a great blessing that the Lord remembered us during His week of suffering."
H.H. Pope Shenouda III

Covenant Thursday

Summary of Covenant Thursday

WHAT DID JESUS DO	VS.	WHAT THE CHURCH DOES TODAY

Jesus and His disciples begin to prepare for the celebration of the Passover.

Jesus warns His Disciples that one of them will betray Him - Judas Iscariot

The Church remembers this event with a procession called the Judas Procession

This procession is done backwards (clockwise) signifies the Church's rejection of Judas and his actions

Jesus washed the feet of His Disciples

How amazing - the Creator of Universe has come to Earth and in humility and true love, he goes on his hands and knees to wash our feet!

The Church celebrates this by the Washing of the Feet (Lakkan)

Like Jesus, Abouna washes our feet as a symbol of repentance

Jesus celebrates the Passover with his disciples, then **establishes the sacrament of the Eucharist.**

The Church remembers this by performing the first and only Divine Liturgy in PassionWeek

Jesus says to his disciples "Do this in remembrance of me" (Luke 22:19) This is where the Great Mystery of the Bread and Wine becoming His Body and Blood in the Liturgy, like Jesus established.

SCAN ME

37

Covenant Thursday

Rites of First Hour/Raising of Morning Incense

- <u>The 1st Hour of Pascha is different today as it combines what is normally read during the 1st Hour of Pascha for Thursday and Matins (Prayers before the Liturgy)</u>
- Abouna raises incense before the altar to prepare for the Liturgy and these prayers are said in the following order:
    - Thanksgiving prayer
    - Verses of cymbals
    - Psalm 51 (Have Mercy upon me)
    - Litanies of the Sick and the Oblations
    - Let us praise with the angels saying..., Holy God (Agios)... who was Born, Holy God... who was Crucified, Holy God who was Crucified...,
    - The Doxologies
    - The Creed
    - Abouna says Efnouti Nai Nan (O God have mercy on us) and the people responding in the long tune of Lord Have Mercy (x3)
    - The Acts, sung in a special mournful tune
    - The Acts read in English.
    - Judas Procession with a special mournful hymn
    - *Trisagion* - Holy God, Holy Mighty, Holy Immortal who was crucified for our sake
    - Litany of the Gospel
    - Readings:Psalm, Gospel and the Commentary of the 1st Hour
- <u>At the conclusion of the 1st hour, the rest of the morning Pascha hours are then prayed up until the end of the 9th hour.</u>

Covenant Thursday

PROCESSION OF JUDAS HYMN

Judas (x6)
Who has broken the law.

With silver you have sold Christ to the Jews, who have broken the law.

The law breakers took Christ and nailed Him on the cross at the Place of the Cranium.

Judas (x6)
Who has broken the law.

Barabbas the condemned thief was set free and the Master, the Judge they crucified. They thrust a spear in Your side, and as a thief they nailed You on the Cross.

They laid You in a tomb. O You who raised Lazarus from the Tomb.

Judas (x6)
Who has broken the law.

For as Jonah stayed three days inside the whale's belly, also our Saviour stayed three days.
After He died, they sealed the tomb.

Judas (x6)
Who has broken the law.

Truly He rose but the soldiers were not aware that truly the Saviour of the world has risen.
He Who suffered and died for our sake, O Lord, glory be to you. Amen.

DID YOU KNOW?
All the Instruments played (the Cymbals and Triangle) are hit inside-out to give a mournful tune of bitterness and rejection of Judas' betrayal of Jesus

Covenant Thursday

Rites of The Liturgy of the Waters (Lakkan)

> "Lakkan" means basin or Container in Arabic

- <u>The Liturgy of the Waters is prayed after the Ninth Hour of Pascha</u>
- <u>The prayers and hymn sung during the Lakkan are prayed in an annual (normal) tune, not in a mournful one</u>
- Abouna and the Deacons put on their Liturgical vestments (Tonia) to start the Liturgy of the Blessing of the Water and these prayers are said in the following order:

  - Thanksgiving Prayer
  - Verses of Cymbals
  - Psalm 51
  - Prophecies, Homily, and Pauline Epistle
  - Trisagion
  - Gospel Litany, Psalm and Gospel
  - Abouna sings Efnouti Nai nan with the people respond in the long tune of Lord Have Mercy (x10)
  - Abouna prays many Litanies and prayers for everyone in Church and for other people in the world.
  - The water is prayed on with special prayers and the people chant "Amen" in response
  - A Deacon then says "Saved. Amen, And with your Spirit."
  - Abouna then prays "Blessed be the Lord Jesus Christ," and the people respond with "One is the All Holy Father...," (Just like in the Liturgy)
  - Psalm 150
  - Abouna washes the feet of the Congregation

Covenant Thursday

Rites of the First Divine Liturgy

This Liturgy is shorter than normal as the Church takes out many prayers and any mention of Christ's death, resurrection and ascension.

The reason for this we are still in the journey of Jesus' Passion and have not reached His Death and Resurrection

During the mass we remember what Christ says, _"This is my Body which is broken for you and for many, to be given for the Remission of Sins, do this in Remembrance of me."_

After partaking of the Holy Body and Blood, the Eleventh Hour of Pascha is prayed.

Jesus said to his disciples, "Do this in remembrance of me."

Covenant Thursday

Summary of Great Friday Eve (Thursday Night)

Known as the <u>Night of Gethsemane</u> – this is important as it was where Jesus taught us to pray even during difficult times. It is also the last place He was before being captured and put on trial.

Thok Te Ti Gom gets longer! *"To you is the Power, the Glory, the Blessing, the Majesty, Forever Amen, My Lord Jesus Christ my Good Saviour, <u>the Lord is my Strength and my praise, He became to</u>*

This is the real beginning of the trial of Jesus to remind us of His Passion and Love for us.

The Prayers are also extra special this night as we start to read <u>Four Gospels every hour instead of only one</u>. Reading of the four gospels continues until the end of Great Friday

PASCHA PRAISE (THOK TE TI GOM)

To you is the Power, the Glory the Blessing, the Majesty forever amen, Emmanuel Our God and Our King.	Thok te ti-gom, nem pi-o-oo nem pi-esmo, nem pi-amhahee sha eneh amen, Emmano-eel pen-nouti pen-oroo.	Ⲑⲱⲕ ⲧⲉ ϯϫⲟⲙ ⲛⲉⲙ ⲡⲓⲱ̀ⲟⲩ ⲛⲉⲙ ⲡⲓⲥ̀ⲙⲟⲩ ⲛⲉⲙ Ⲡⲓⲁ̀ⲙⲁϩⲓ ϣⲁ ⲉ̀ⲛⲉϩ ⲁ̀ⲙⲏⲛ: Ⲉⲙⲙⲁⲛⲟⲩⲏⲗ ⲡⲉⲛⲛⲟⲩϯ ⲡⲉⲛⲟⲩⲣⲟ.
To you is the Power, the Glory the Blessing, the Majesty forever amen, My Lord Jesus Christ. My Good Saviour. The Lord is my Strength and my Praise, He became to me a Holy Salvation.	Thok te ti-gom, nem pi-o-oo nem pi-esmo, nem pi-amhahee sha eneh amen, pa-Shois Esos Piekh-restos. Pasoteer en-aghathos. Ta-gom, nem pa-esmo pi-epshois af-shobi nee, af-soteria ef-owab.	Ⲑⲱⲕ ⲧⲉ ϯϫⲟⲙ ⲛⲉⲙ ⲡⲓⲱ̀ⲟⲩ ⲛⲉⲙ ⲡⲓⲥ̀ⲙⲟⲩ ⲛⲉⲙ Ⲡⲓⲁ̀ⲙⲁϩⲓ ϣⲁ ⲉ̀ⲛⲉϩ ⲁ̀ⲙⲏⲛ: Ⲡⲁⲟ̅ⲥ̅ Ⲓⲏ̅ⲥ̅ Ⲡ̅ⲭ̅ⲥ̅: ⲡⲁⲥⲱⲧⲏⲣ ⲛ̀ⲁ̀ⲅⲁⲑⲟⲥ: ⲧⲁϫⲟⲙ ⲛⲉⲙ ⲡⲁⲥ̀ⲙⲟⲩ ⲡⲉ Ⲡⲟ̅ⲥ̅ ⲁϥϣⲱⲡⲓ ⲛⲏⲓ ⲉⲩⲥⲱⲧⲏⲣⲓⲁ̀ ⲉϥⲟⲩⲁⲃ.
To you is the Power, the Glory the Blessing, the Majesty forever amen.	Thok te ti-gom, nem pi-o-oo nem pi-esmo,nem pi-amhahee sha eneh amen.	Ⲑⲱⲕ ⲧⲉ ϯϫⲟⲙ ⲛⲉⲙ ⲡⲓⲱ̀ⲟⲩ ⲛⲉⲙ ⲡⲓⲥ̀ⲙⲟⲩ ⲛⲉⲙ Ⲡⲓⲁ̀ⲙⲁϩⲓ ϣⲁ ⲉ̀ⲛⲉϩ ⲁ̀ⲙⲏⲛ.

"To you is the Power, the Glory the Blessing, the Majesty forever. Amen."

Covenant Thursday

<u>Spot the Difference!</u>

Circle 12 Differences in the images of Jesus washing the Disciples feet.

Covenant Thursday

```
V Y U Q D Z E P R E T S A M B L N
H U N O H V Y D X W H W A D S X C
F V O A M X A R L H R T W A E H P
J L M C E E B B Z W I N E R L E O
B F G E R L K D G M F V V E P R N
V A T V Y S C Y A A O A H B I X M
D D W F A F A V R E T E P M C F F
L I E D W R G U E T A E Y E S U A
T E U A T W P W K T Z G I M I J Z
T J T E O Q Y E A E D S V E D P Z
E E B L T E V M T W P U S R R A T
R B L V Q R N L K D F E R N E S M
S O Y W E Q R X P V R B I J H S U
F E B S I U X H I V Q R A F C O H
V G N O K O Q R A M X R H E A V I
C N A Y D T H N O W X V L M E E G
R A Q A R Y T Z H D E V O L T R C
```

WORDBANK
Remember Servant Bread Teacher Disciples Betray
Eat Blood Water Feet Clean Take Body Peter
Judas Loved Serve Wine Master Passover Follow

GREAT FRIDAY

"His love towards us reaches its peak when He offered and sacrificed himself when He gave his life for ransom for many for the redemption of sins" H.H. Pope Shenouda III

Great Friday

Summary of Great Friday

<u>By far this is one of the most important days in Pascha!!</u>
There are so many more prayers, reading and hymns which are said and chanted than any day in the Coptic year.
This is because our Saviour, the perfect sacrifice, was crucified to save us.

1st Hour: Jesus begins his trial and lies are said about Him. Jesus is taken to Pilate.

3rd Hour: Pilate washes his hands. Soliders take Jesus, whip Him and make fun of Him. They dress Him in a scarlet robe, place a crown of thorns on His head and place a reed in His hands.

6th Hour: <u>Jesus is crucified.</u> We remember the Right Hand Thief.

9th Hour: Jesus dies on the cross.

11th Hour: Jesus is taken down from the cross.

12th Hour: Jesus is buried.

SCAN ME

Great Friday

Summary of 6th Hour of Great Friday

In this hour, we focus **ONLY** on the Crucified Christ!

The most powerful reading of the week, is in this hour, where we read a part of Isaiah. Chapter 53, where Jesus is described as The Lamb. He also prophesies about His crucifixion, the burial and the resurrection.

St. Paul in his epistle to the Galations writes, "I pride myself only in the Cross of our Lord Jesus Christ" (Galatians 6:14). He teaches us that the cross is a crown of victory and we should take pride in the cross because it has redeemed all mankind.

At the end of the 6th hour, we read in the Gospel of Matthew, that the earth was filled with darkness, ""_there was darkness over all the land" (Matthew 27:45)_ . The church commemorates this by turning off all candles and the lights.

Great Friday

Rites of 6th Hour of Great Friday

At the 6th hour the Deacons put on their Tonias and their Badreshen – but guess what, they use the other side which is usually blue or purple to signify sadness!

- There are a number of hymns sung in this hour that you may know, but will sound different including:
  a. The hymn of the censor (Tai-Shori) – becomes longer and sounds sadder than when we normally sing it
  b. The hymn of the cross (Fai-etafenf)
  c. The Pauline Epistle – becomes longer and sounds sadder

- These hymns are followed by:
  o Litanies of the Sixth Hour
  o The Greek hymn *Omonogenes*, (O Only Begotten..)
  o Trisagion in the mournful tune.
  o Psalm and Gospel
  o Exposition
  o Litanies
  o *Kyrie eleson* (x3) in a long tune
  o The Right Hand Thief's Hymn (Remember Me O Lord)

Great Friday

6TH HOUR LITANY

O You who on the sixth day, and in the sixth hour, was nailed to the cross for the sin which our father Adam dared to commit in Paradise; tear the handwriting of oursins, O Christ our God and save us.

Glory to the Father, and to the Son, and the Holy Spirit.	Zoxa Patri kei Eio, ke ageio Epnevmati	Ⲇⲟⲝⲁ Ⲡⲁⲧⲣⲓ ⲕⲉ Ⲩⲓⲱ̀ ⲕⲉ ⲁ̀ⲅⲓⲱ̀ Ⲡⲛⲁⲧⲓ.
Now and ever and unto the ages of the ages. Amen.	Ke neen ke a-ee ke estos e-onas-ton e-onon. Amen.	Ⲕⲉ ⲛⲩⲛ ⲕⲉ ⲁ̀ⲓ ⲕⲉ ⲓⲥⲧⲟⲩⲥ ⲉ̀ⲱ̀ⲛⲁⲥ ⲧⲱⲛ ⲉ̀ⲱ̀ⲛⲱⲛ ⲁ̀ⲙⲏⲛ.

THE HYMN OF THE TRISAGION

Holy God, Holy Mighty, Holy Immortal, who was crucified for us, have mercy upon us.
Holy God, Holy Mighty, Holy Immortal, who was crucified for us, have mercy upon us.
Holy God, Holy Mighty, Holy Immortal, who was crucified for us, have mercy upon us.

Glory to the Father, and to the Son, and the Holy Spirit.	Zoxa Patri kei Eio, ke ageio Epnevmati	Ⲇⲟⲝⲁ Ⲡⲁⲧⲣⲓ ⲕⲉ Ⲩⲓⲱ̀ ⲕⲉ ⲁ̀ⲅⲓⲱ̀ Ⲡⲛⲁⲧⲓ.
Now and ever and unto the ages of the ages. Amen. OHoly Trinity, have mercy upon us.	Ke neen ke a-ee ke estos e-onas-ton e-onon. Amen. Ageya trias, elee-eson emas.	Ⲕⲉ ⲛⲩⲛ ⲕⲉ ⲁ̀ⲓ ⲕⲉ ⲓⲥⲧⲟⲩⲥ ⲉ̀ⲱ̀ⲛⲁⲥ ⲧⲱⲛ ⲉ̀ⲱ̀ⲛⲱⲛ ⲁ̀ⲙⲏⲛ. Ⲁ̀ⲅⲓⲁ Ⳍⲣⲓⲁⲥ: ⲉ̀ⲗⲉⲏⲥⲟⲛ ⲏ̀ⲙⲁⲥ.

O ONLY BEGOTTEN

DID YOU KNOW?
This hymn reminds us of our faith, like the Creed. This hymn has an unknown author.
<u>Believe it or not!</u>
This hymn is sung during the ordination of a new Pope!

O Only Begotten Word of God, Eternal, and Immortal, Who for our salvation did accept all sufferings, Who was incarnate of the Holy Theotokos, Mother of God (and Ever Virgin Mary) x2.

Who, without change, became Man and was crucified, Christ, God. Who trampled down death by death. One of the Holy Trinity, Who is glorified with the Father and the Holy Spirit, Save us.

Holy God, who being God, for our sake, became Man without change. Holy Mighty, who by weakness showed forth what is greater than power. Holy Immortal, who was crucified for our sake, and endured death in His flesh, the Eternal and Immortal.

O Holy Trinity, have mercy on us.

CONFESSION OF THE RIGHT HAND THIEF

Remember me O Lord, when You come into Your kingdom.	Aripa-meve o Pa-shois, ak-shan-ee khen tek-metooro.	Ⲁⲣⲓⲡⲁⲙⲉⲛⲓ ⲱⲠⲁϬⲟⲓⲥ: ⲁⲕϣⲁⲛⲓ ϧⲉⲛ ⲦⲉⲔⲙⲉⲦⲟⲩⲣⲟ.
Rememeber me O King, when You come into Your kingdom.	Aripa-meve o Pa-oooro, ak-shan-ee khen tek-metooro.	Ⲁⲣⲓⲡⲁⲙⲉⲛⲓ ⲱⲠⲁⲟⲩⲣⲟ: ⲁⲕϣⲁⲛⲓ ϧⲉⲛ ⲦⲉⲔⲙⲉⲦⲟⲩⲣⲟ.
Remember me O Holy One, when You come into Your kingdom.	Aripa-meve o Fe-eth-owab, ak-shan-ee khen tek-metooro.	Ⲁⲣⲓⲡⲁⲙⲉⲛⲓ ⲱⲪⲏⲉⲑⲟⲩⲁⲃ: ⲁⲕϣⲁⲛⲓ ϧⲉⲛ ⲦⲉⲔⲙⲉⲦⲟⲩⲣⲟ.
Holy God, Holy Mighty, Holy Immortal, who was crucified for us, have mercy on us.	Je agios O Theos, Agios les-shero, Agios Athanatos, o estavrotees dee mas.	Ⲭⲉ ⲁⲅⲓⲟⲥ ⲟⲐⲉⲟⲥ: ⲁⲅⲓⲟⲥ ⲓⲥⲭⲩⲣⲟⲥ: ⲁⲅⲓⲟⲥ ⲁⲑⲁⲛⲁⲧⲟⲥ: ⲟ ⲉⲥⲧⲁⲩⲣⲱⲑⲓⲥ Ⲇⲓ ⲏⲙⲁⲥ ⲉⲗⲉⲏⲥⲟⲛ ⲏⲙⲁⲥ.
Glory to the Father, and to the Son, and to the Holy Spirit. Now and ever and unto the ages of the ages. Amen.	Zoxa Patri kei Eio, ke ageio Epnevmati, ke neen ke a-ee ke estos e-onas-ton e-onon. Amen.	Ⲇⲟⲝⲁ Ⲡⲁⲧⲣⲓ ⲕⲉ Ⲧⲓⲱ ⲕⲉ ⲁⲅⲓⲱ Ⲡⲛⲁⲧⲓ. Ⲕⲉ ⲛⲩⲛ ⲕⲉ ⲁⲓ ⲕⲉ ⲓⲥⲧⲟⲩⲥ ⲉⲱⲛⲁⲥ Ⲧⲱⲛ ⲉⲱⲛⲱⲛ ⲁⲙⲏⲛ.

Great Friday

Summary of 9th Hour of Great Friday

In the 9th Hour, Jesus cried out in Aramaic (the language Jesus spoke) a number of well-known sentences while on the Cross.

This is the hour when our Savior bowed His head and died on the Cross.
The church teaches us that this is the ultimate sacrifice of love!

- During this hour, an earthquake happened and the veil of the temple was torn in two.
- This hour is also the moment:
  - the devil was terrified and tied up
  - those who slept in hope rejoiced
  - right hand thief entered paradise
  - the time that Longinus, a roman soldier thrust the spear into the side of Our Lord, and He bled blood and water

DID YOU KNOW?
Longinus became a martyr after witnessing this majestic event!

Rites of 9th Hour of Great Friday

- We begin the 9th hour by switching all the lights back on
- Abouna raises incense in front of the icon of the crucifixion
- The deacons begin chanting in a mournful tune the hymns of:
  - Tee-shori (is different from Tai Shori),
  - Fai-etafenf,
  - Pauline in Coptic or English.
  - Litanies
  - Trisagion

9TH HOUR LITANY

O You who tasted death in the flesh in the ninth hourfor our sake, we the sinners, put to death our carnal lusts; O Christ our God and save us.

Glory to the Father, and to the Son, and the Holy Spirit	Zoxa Patri kei Eio, ke ageio Epnevmati	Ⲇⲟⲝⲁ Ⲡⲁⲧⲣⲓ ⲕⲉ Ⲩⲓⲱ̀ ⲕⲉ ⲁ̀ⲅⲓⲱ̀ Ⲡⲛ̅ⲁ̅ⲧⲓ.
Now and ever and unto the ages of the ages. Amen.	Ke neen ke a-ee ke estos e-onaston e-onon. Amen.	Ⲕⲉ ⲛⲩⲛ ⲕⲉ ⲁ̀ⲓ ⲕⲉ ⲓⲥⲧⲟⲩⲥ ⲉ̀ⲱ̀ⲛⲁⲥ ⲧⲱⲛ ⲉ̀ⲱ̀ⲛⲱⲛ ⲁ̀ⲙⲏⲛ.

DID YOU KNOW?
We repeat this litany at the 9th hour in the Agpeya.

Great Friday

FILL IN THE BLANKS

1st Prophecy
A Reading from the Book of Jeremiah the Prophet.
"I was like an innocent _____ led to be sacrificed. They plotted an _____ device against me, saying, 'Come let us put wood in His bread, and destroy him _____ and _____ from the land of living, so his _____ might not be remembered any longer.'"
(Jeremiah 11:17-12:13)

Psalm of 9th Hour
"_____ me, O God; for the waters have come in to my soul. I am stuck in the mire of the sea and there is no _____ to stand. They gave me gall for my _____, and they gave me vinegar for my _____." Alleluia
(Psalm 69:1-2)

1st Gospel of 9th Hour
"My _____, my _____, why have you_____ (left) me?"
(Matthew 27:46-50)

2nd Gospel of 9th Hour
"And at the _____ hour Jesus cried out with a loud voice saying, 'Eloi, Eloi lama sabachthani?' which is translated: My _____, My _____, why have you _____ me."
(Mark 15:34-37)

3rd Gospel of 9th Hour
"Then the sun was _____, and the veil of the _____ was rent in the midst."
(Luke 23:45-46)

4th Gospel of 9th Hour
"So Jesus had recieved the sour wine, He said, It is _____ and he bowing His head, He gave up His _____."
(John 19:28-30)

Great Friday

Summary of 12th Hour of Great Friday

This is the <u>first time</u> in the week that pray the 12th hour during the Pascha. This hour commemorates the burial of Christ.

The 12th hour is both mournful and joyful because we recognise that Christ died for our sins but are also joyful because through his death and resurrection, He saved us from sin.

To understand how people during Jesus' time buried the dead, we need to understand both Jewish and Roman traditions

<u>ROMAN BURIAL</u>　　VS.　　<u>JEWISH BURIAL</u>

| leave the crucified bodies on the cross for the birds | throw the body in a pit where garbage and sewerage are to be burnt |

However, with Jesus, two important people prepared Jesus for his burial. They were <u>Joseph of Arimathea</u> and <u>Nicodemeus.</u>

| Joseph asked Pilate to take Jesus' body | Nicodemus bought fine linen, perfume and spices to anoint Jesus' body |

Something special happens during this hour!

Abouna re-enacts the burial of Christ while we sing a special hymn called Golgotha.

Abouna places an icon of the burial and a cross in a white linen sheet on the altar. Just like Jesus' body was anointed, red rose petals, spices and perfume are also added on the icon and the cross. Two candles are lit on each side to represent the two angels at the tomb.

Rites of 12th Hour of Great Friday

- At this point in time, the curtains and banners in the church that are black, are changed to white.
- Now the deacons and Abouna enter into the altar and these prayers are said in the following order:
  - Prophecy (Lamentations of Jeremiah)
  - Paschal Praise (Thok Te Ti Gom)
  - Psalm, Gospel and Exposition
  - Litanies

Guess what?

- The congregation then sings _Kyrie eleison 400 times_, along with metanias (Prostrations)
  - 100 Kyrie eleison are done in each direction, starting from the east (facing the altar) then west, then north, then ending with south. How exhausting!

- Abouna and the deacons do a procession around the altar three times, then three times around the entire church and ending with one final procession in the altar.
- Golgotha is sung
- All 150 psalms are read
- Concluding blessing

DID YOU KNOW?

We say 100 Kyrie Eleison, as it is a large round number which shows our infinite prayers for mercy and forgiveness.

Saying them in the 4 compass points shows that we worship God, who is everywhere!

GOLGOTHA

> **DID YOU KNOW?**
> The music to the hymn of Golgotha was sung by the ancient Egyptians. They used it during the burial ceremonies. The church took the music and changed the lyrics.

"Golgotha" in Hebrew, "Kranion" in Greek, the place where You were crucified Lord. You spread out Your hands, and two thieves were crucified with you; at Your right, and at Your left, You in the middle, O Good Saviour.

Glory to the Father, and to the Son, and to the Holy Spirit. The thief at Your right cried out saying: "Remember me, O my Lord; remember me, O my Saviour, remember me, O my King, when You come into Your Kingdom."

The Lord answered him in a gentle voice saying; "Today you shall be with Me in My Kingdom." Now and ever and unto the ages of the ages. Amen.

The righteous Joseph and Nicodemus came and took the flesh of Christ, embalmed Him, prepared Him, put Him in a tomb, singing to Him saying, "Holy God, Holy Mighty, Holy Immortal, who was crucified for us, have mercy upon us."

Glory to the Father, and to the Son, and to the Holy Spirit. Now and ever and unto the ages of the ages. Amen.

Let us also worship Him crying out saying: "Have mercy on us, God our Saviour, who was crucified on the cross trampled Satan under our feet."

Save us and have mercy on us. Lord have mercy, Lord have mercy, Lord bless us. Amen. Bless me; bless me. Lo, the metanoia. Forgive me. Say the blessing.

Great Friday

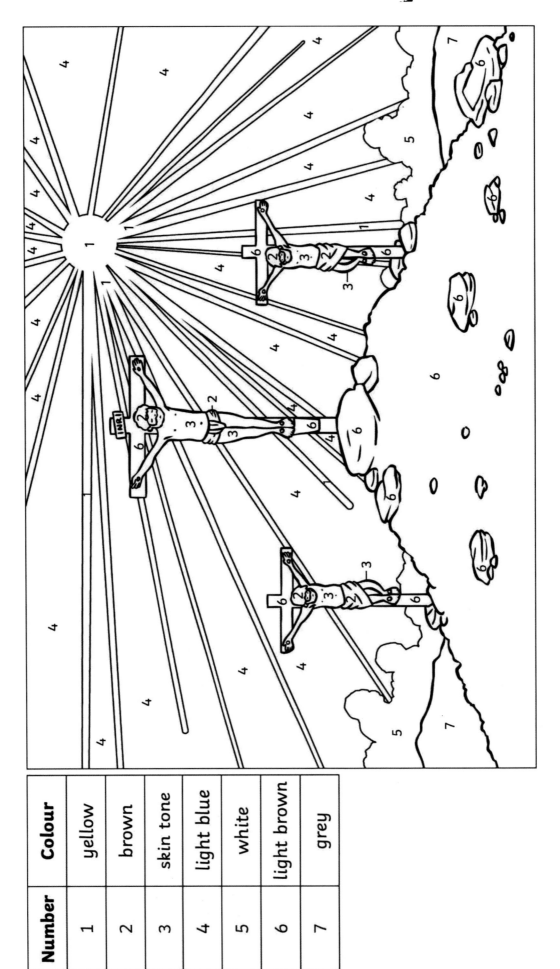

Number	Colour
1	yellow
2	brown
3	skin tone
4	light blue
5	white
6	light brown
7	grey

Great Friday

G O L G O T H A X U T
Q W E R T Y U I D I R
M L A S P K L S F O L
M N V C X E J B G P O
S S U M E D O C I N P
L Z F T T Q S S H G E
E X G G G Q E A D V R
G C J F H W P D G F F
N V L D K E H F H X U
A N K A D R S G J C M
Q M O S S L W H K V E
W H I F A W D O L J L
E D U I D F S D M A K
R S R F F G A G A E J
T U Y H Q G A D S F N
B T H U O S P I C E S

WORDBANK
Burial Spices Golgotha Angels Psalm
Perfume Joseph Nicodemus Women

JOYOUS
SATURDAY

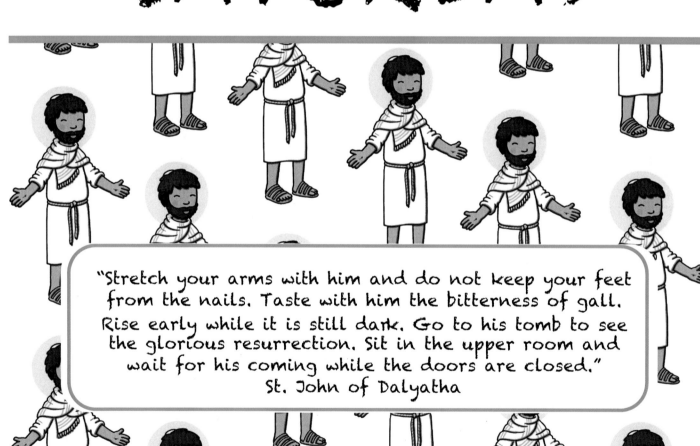

"Stretch your arms with him and do not keep your feet
from the nails. Taste with him the bitterness of gall.
Rise early while it is still dark. Go to his tomb to see
the glorious resurrection. Sit in the upper room and
wait for his coming while the doors are closed."
St. John of Dalyatha

Joyous Saturday

Summary of Joyous Saturday

This is the day that Christ descended into Hades to free the righteous souls that were in bondage by Satan.

We begin the service after the long day we had on Great Friday! We go from late on Friday night to early morning on Saturday, finishing with a Liturgy. This is called the "Night of the Apocalypse."

DID YOU KNOW?
The word *Apoghalamsees (Arabic)* takes its origin from the Greek word "Apocalypse."
The word itself means "vision" or "revelation"

Going to church in the darkness of the night symbolises sin and death and why we leave the church in the morning, is because we leave sin behind and celebrate Joyous Saturday.

During this service we sing midnight praises and many wonderful hymns to both mourn the death of Christ and rejoice for our salvation.
If you pay very close attention, the hymns are sung both in the <u>sad and normal tune throughout the night.</u>

All the prayers and prophecies of this night remind us of Christ in the Tomb and salvation.

Another important book from the bible is read! The WHOLE book of **Revelations!**

We do this as it symbolises and gives us hope of Christ's second coming.

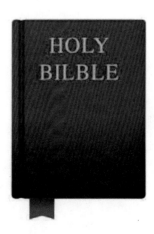

Joyous Saturday

Rites of Joyous Saturday

If you missed out on Great Friday and have come to church this late at night, something in the church has changed!

The black curtain in front of the altar and all other black banners hanging around the church have been taken down and replaced by white ones!
This reminds us of the victorious church in Paradise

- These prayers during the night are said in the following order:
    - Psalm 151
    - Procession around the church – the deacons chant the exposition of the Second Canticle
    - First Canticle
    - Old Testament prayers
    - Third Canticle
    - O Sing unto him who was crucified... (Aripsalin)
    - Tenen (Greek hymn about the three young youth in the fiery furnace)
    - New testament praises and prophecies are read
    - Another procession around the church
    - <u>Matins</u>
    - 3rd and 6th hour of Joyous Satuday
    - Revelation
    - 9th Hour of Joyous Saturday
    - <u>The night is ended with the Liturgy</u>

Joyous Saturday

PSALM 151

I am small among my brothers: and a boy in my father's house: I tended my father's sheep. My hands made an organ: and my fingers tuned a psaltery: Alleluia (x3)

And who shall tell my Lord? He is the Lord: He listens to everyone that cries to Him He sent for His angels, and took me from my father's sheep: and anointed me with His anointing oil: Alleluia (x3)

My brothers are handsome and great. But the Lord did not take pleasure in them, I went out to meet the philistine: and he cursed me with his idols: Alleluia (x3)

But I drew his sword which he had, and beheaded him.

And removed reproach from the children of Israel. Alleluia (x3)

Glory be to Our God. Again Glory be to Our God.

THIRD CANTICLE (HOAS)

Blessed are You, O Lord, God of our Fathers, and exceedingly to be blessed, and exalted above all forever.

Blessed is Your Holy Name and Your Glory, and exceedingly to be blessed, and exalted forever.

Blessed are You in the holy temple of Your Glory, and exceedingly to be praised, and exalted above all forever.

Blessed are You who beholds the depths and sits upon the Cherubim, and exceedingly to be blessed, and exalted above all forever.

Blessed are You on the Throne of Your Kingdom, and exceedingly to be blessed and exalted above all forever.

Blessed are You in the firmament of heaven, and exceedingly to be blessed, and exalted above all forever.

Joyous Saturday

THIRD CANTICLE (HOAS)

Bless the Lord all you works of the Lord, praise Him and exalt Him above all forever.	Evlogi-te pan-ta-ta ergha, Kerie-ton ke-rion emni-te, ke epe-rip-sote avton, yes toos e-o-nas.	Ⲉⲩⲗⲟⲅⲓⲧⲉ ⲡⲁⲛⲧⲁⲧⲁ ⲉⲣⲅⲁ: Ⲕⲩⲣⲓⲉ ⲧⲟⲛ Ⲕⲩⲣⲓⲟⲛ ⲩⲙⲛⲓⲧⲉ: ⲕⲉ ⲩⲡⲉⲣⲩⲯⲟⲧⲉ ⲁⲩⲧⲟⲛ: ⲓⲥ ⲧⲟⲩⲥ ⲉⲱⲛⲁⲥ.

Praise Him, glorify Him, and exalt Him, His mercy is forever. For He is praised, glorified, and exalted above the ages, His mercy is forever.

Bless the Lord, O heaven, Praise Him and exalt Him above all forever.

Bless the Lord, all you angels of the Lord, Praise Him and exalt Him above all forever.

Bless the Lord, all you waters above the heaven, Praise Him and exalt Him above all forever.

Bless the Lord all you works of the Lord, praise Him and exalt Him above all forever.	Evlogi-te pan-ta-ta ergha, Kerie-ton ke-rion emni-te, ke epe-rip-sote avton, yes toos e-o-nas.	Ⲉⲩⲗⲟⲅⲓⲧⲉ ⲡⲁⲛⲧⲁⲧⲁ ⲉⲣⲅⲁ: Ⲕⲩⲣⲓⲉ ⲧⲟⲛ Ⲕⲩⲣⲓⲟⲛ ⲩⲙⲛⲓⲧⲉ: ⲕⲉ ⲩⲡⲉⲣⲩⲯⲟⲧⲉ ⲁⲩⲧⲟⲛ: ⲓⲥ ⲧⲟⲩⲥ ⲉⲱⲛⲁⲥ.

Praise Him, glorify Him, and exalt Him, His mercy is forever. For He is praised, glorified, and exalted above the ages, His mercy is forever.

Bless the Lord, all you powers of the Lord, Praise Him and exalt Him above all forever.

Bless the Lord, O Sun and Moon, Praise Him and exalt Him above all forever.

Bless the Lord, all you stars of heaven, Praise Him and exalt Him above all forever.

Joyous Saturday

Bless the Lord all you works of the Lord, praise Him and exalt Him above all forever.	Evlogi-te pan-ta-ta ergha, Kerie-ton ke-rion emni-te, ke epe-rip-sote avton, yes toos e-o-nas.	Ⲉⲩⲗⲟⲅⲓⲧⲉ ⲡⲁⲛⲧⲁⲧⲁ ⲉⲣⲅⲁ: Ⲕⲩⲣⲓⲉ̀ ⲧⲟⲛ Ⲕⲩⲣⲓⲟⲛ ⲩ̀ⲙⲛⲓⲧⲉ: ⲕⲉ ⲩ̀ⲡⲉⲣⲩⲯⲟⲧⲉ ⲁⲩⲧⲟⲛ: ⲓⲥ ⲧⲟⲩⲥ ⲉ̀ⲱ̀ⲛⲁⲥ.

Praise Him, glorify Him, and exalt Him, His mercy is forever. For He is praised, glorified, and exalted above the ages, His mercy is forever.

Bless the Lord, O you rain and dew, Praise Him and exalt Him above all forever.

Bless the Lord, O you clouds and winds, Praise Him and exalt Him above all forever.

Bless the Lord, all you spirits, Praise Him and exalt Him above all forever.

Bless the Lord all you works of the Lord, praise Him and exalt Him above all forever.	Evlogi-te pan-ta-ta ergha, Kerie-ton ke-rion emni-te, ke epe-rip-sote avton, yes toos e-o-nas.	Ⲉⲩⲗⲟⲅⲓⲧⲉ ⲡⲁⲛⲧⲁⲧⲁ ⲉⲣⲅⲁ: Ⲕⲩⲣⲓⲉ̀ ⲧⲟⲛ Ⲕⲩⲣⲓⲟⲛ ⲩ̀ⲙⲛⲓⲧⲉ: ⲕⲉ ⲩ̀ⲡⲉⲣⲩⲯⲟⲧⲉ ⲁⲩⲧⲟⲛ: ⲓⲥ ⲧⲟⲩⲥ ⲉ̀ⲱ̀ⲛⲁⲥ.

Praise Him, glorify Him, and exalt Him, His mercy is forever. For He is praised, glorified, and exalted above the ages, His mercy is forever.

Bless the Lord, O fire and heat, Praise Him and exalt Him above all forever.

Bless the Lord, O cold and heat, Praise Him and exalt Him above all forever.

Bless the Lord, O dew and winds, Praise Him and exalt Him above all forever.

Joyous Saturday

THIRD CANTICLE (HOAS)

Bless the Lord all you works of the Lord, praise Him and exalt Him above all forever.	Evlogi-te pan-ta-ta ergha, Kerie-ton ke-rion emni-te, ke epe-rip-sote avton, yes toos e-o-nas.	Ⲉⲩⲗⲟⲅⲓⲧⲉ ⲡⲁⲛⲧⲁⲧⲁ ⲉⲣⲅⲁ: Ⲕⲩⲣⲓⲉ ⲧⲟⲛ Ⲕⲩⲣⲓⲟⲛ ⲩⲙⲛⲓⲧⲉ: ⲕⲉ ⲩ̀ⲡⲉⲣⲩⲯⲟⲧⲉ ⲁⲩⲧⲟⲛ: ⲓⲥ ⲧⲟⲩⲥ ⲉ̀ⲱ̀ⲛⲁⲥ.
Praise Him, glorify Him, and exalt Him, His mercy is forever. For He is praised, glorified, and exalted above the ages, His mercy is forever.		

THE HYMN OF BRIGHT SATURDAY

Praise the name of the holy God/ To Him is due praise and Glory/ The Saviour whom we now all laid/ Agios Athanatos Nai Nan

In wisdom He had determined/ To save us from adversity/ Humbled Himself as a servant/ Agios Athanatos Nai Nan

A True human He did become/ And took the form of the earthly/ While still in His Father's bosom/ Agios Athanatos Nai Nan

Two natures united in Him/ Divinity and Humanity/ Let us glorify with this Hymns/ Agios Athanatos Nai Nan

Mary has carried the Praised/ In her womb, nine months fully/ Angles chanted and proclaimed/ Agios Athanatos Nai Nan

The Master came to save Adam/ After he lived in misery/ His great love we cannot fathom/ Agios Athanatos Nai Nan

Immortal and everlasting/ Turned water to wine mysteriously/ Accepted death on the cross hanging/ Agios Athanatos Nai Nan

Kind, merciful, and compassionate/ To whom is due all the glory/ Dwelt in Mary our advocate/ Agios Athanatos Nai Nan

Joyous Saturday

THE HYMN OF BRIGHT SATURDAY

Adam's shame He abolished/ By dwelling in our lady/ Our Salvation He accomplished/ Agios Athanatos Nai Nan

The Son of God indeed His name/ Was also Son of Man truly/ Uniting two natures He came/ Agios Athanatos Nai Nan

The Cherubim and the Seraphim/ Were witnessed praising joyfully/ Proclaiming and worshipping Him/ Agios Athanatos Nai Nan

The scholars were truly amazed/ Pondered upon Virgin Mary/ The Second Heaven who is praised/ Agios Athanatos Nai Nan

From David's house shone the Bright Light/ Mankind led by the Almighty/ Ranks of heaven worship in might/ Agios Athanatos Nai Nan

Was incarnate to save mankind/ Commanded us not to worry/ May he fill our souls and mind/ Agios Athanatos Nai Nan

HE WHO HAS AN EAR

He who has an ear to hear let him hear, what the Spirit says to the churches.

THE TWELVE TRIBES

From the tribe of Judah twelve thousand were sealed;
From the tribe of Reuben twelve thousand were sealed;
From the tribe of Gad twelve thousand were sealed;

From the tribe of Asher twelve thousand were sealed;
From the tribe of Naphtali twelve thousand were sealed;
From the tribe of Manasseh twelve thousand were sealed;

From the tribe of Simeon twelve thousand were sealed;
From the tribe of Levi twelve thousand were sealed; From
the tribe of Issachar twelve thousand were sealed;

From the tribe of Zebulun twelve thousand were sealed;
From the tribe of Joseph twelve thousand were sealed;
From the tribe of Benjamin twelve thousand were
sealed.

THE HYMN OF THE TRISAGION

Holy God, Holy Mighty, Holy Immortal, who was
crucified for us, have mercy upon us.

Holy God, Holy Mighty, Holy Immortal, who was
crucified for us, have mercy upon us.

Holy God, Holy Mighty, Holy Immortal, who was
crucified for us, have mercy upon us.

Glory to the Father, and to the Son, and the Holy Spirit.	Zoxa Patri kei Eio, ke ageio Epnevmati	Ⲇⲟⲝⲁ Ⲡⲁⲧⲣⲓ ⲕⲉ Ⲩⲓⲱ̀ ⲕⲉ ⲁ̀ⲅⲓⲱ̀ Ⲡⲛⲁⲧⲓ.
Now and ever and unto the ages of the ages. Amen. O Holy Trinity, have mercy upon us.	Ke neen ke'a-ee ke estos e-onas-ton e-onon. Amen. Ageya trias, elee-eson emas.	Ⲕⲉ ⲛⲩⲛ ⲕⲉ ⲁ̀ⲓ ⲕⲉ ⲓⲥⲧⲟⲩⲥ ⲉ̀ⲱ̀ⲛⲁⲥ ⲧⲱⲛ ⲉ̀ⲱ̀ⲛⲱⲛ ⲁ̀ⲙⲏⲛ. Ⲁ̀ⲅⲓⲁ Ⲧⲣⲓⲁⲥ: ⲉ̀ⲗⲉ̀ⲏ̀ⲥⲟⲛ ⲏ̀ⲙⲁⲥ.

Joyous Saturday

PSALM

From the Psalms of our father David the Prophet and King. May his blessings be with us. Amen.

<u>Psalm 3:5,3 and Psalm 82:8</u>

I lay down and slept; I awoke, for the Lord sustained me. But You, O Lord, are a shield for me, My glory and the one lifts up my head.

Arise O God, judge the earth; For you shall inherit all nationsAlleluia.

GOSPEL

O God have mercy and compassion upon us and make us worthy to hear to the Holy Gospel. A reading according to St. Matthew. May his blessings be with us all. Amen.

<u>Matthew 28:1-20</u>

Now after the Sabbath, as the first day of the week began to dawn, Mary Magdalene and the other Mary came to see the tomb. And behold, there was a great earthquake; for an angel of the Lord descended from heaven, and came and rolled back the stone from the door, and sat on it. His countenance was like lightning, and his clothing as white as snow. And the guards shook for fear of him, and became like dead men. But the angel answered and said to the women, "Do not be afraid, for I know that you seek Jesus who was crucified. He is not here; for He is risen, as He said.

Come, see the place where the Lord lay. And go quickly and tell His disciples that He is risen from the dead, and indeed He is going before you into Galilee; there you will see Him. Behold, I have told you. So they went out quickly from the tomb with fear and great joy, and ran to bring His disciples word. And as they went to tell His disciples, behold, Jesus met them, saying, "Rejoice!" So they came and held Him by the feet and worshiped Him. Then Jesus said to them, "Do not be afraid. Go and tell My brethren to go to Galilee, and there they will see Me." Now while they were going, behold, some of the guard came into the city and reported to the chief priests all the things that had happened. When they had assembled with the elders and consulted together, they gave a large sum ofmoney to the soldiers, saying, "Tell them, 'His disciples came at night and stole Him away while we slept.' And if this comes to the governor's ears, we will appease him and make you secure."

Joyous Saturday

GOSPEL

So they took the money and did as they were instructed; and this saying is commonly reported among the Jews until this day. Then the eleven disciples went away into Galilee, to the mountain which Jesus had appointed for them. When they saw Him, they worshiped Him; but some doubted. And Jesus came and spoke to them, saying, "All authority has been given to Me in heaven and on earth. Go therefore and make disciples of all the nations, baptizing them in the name of the Father and of the Son and of the Holy Spirit, teaching them to observe all things that I have commanded you; and lo, I am with you always, even to the end of the age." Amen.

Bow down before the Holy Gospel.
Glory be to God forever.

MY GOD MY GOD – COMMUNION HYMN

My God my God attend to me. Why have You forsaken me? All the words of my transgressions are far away from my salvation.

Joyous Saturday

Challenge!!
Some of the information can be found in your Pascha Book.

ACROSS →
4. What did God give us on the night of Joyous Saturday
7. The book that we read from beginning to end on Joyous Saturday
9. She was wrongly accused of a crime and sentenced to death, but was saved by God
10. Where Christ remained for 3 days
11. This man was a prophet, and his book contains the story of Susanna

DOWN ↓
1. He was in the belly of the fish for 3 days
2. Three young men were sentenced to death in a fiery _____
3. A prophet who was taken up to heaven in a fiery chariot
5. The mother of Samuel
6. This man was a king, and he built the temple
8. This man defeated Goliath

REFERENCES

Aboseif, A.A, 2000. Coptic Hymns. 1st ed. California: Saint Anthony Coptic Orthodox Church.

Awad, Meena. (2014). Teens Guide for Holy Week: St. Shenouda Monastery. ChristianClipart.net. [online] Available at: http://www.christiancliparts.net/index.php?home=1 [Accessed 15 April 2021].

Coloring pages. [online] Available at: http://www.supercoloring.com/coloring-pages/ [Accessed 17 March 2021].

Copts, S.U.S, 2010. *Services of the Decons.* 1st ed. Southern United States: Coptic Orthodox Diocese of the Southern United States

Get Drawings. [online] Available at: http://getdrawings.com/ [Accessed 14 April 2021].

Guide to the Holy Pascha Week. [online] Available at: http://stminachampaign.org/uploads/3/4/4/7/34471607/guide-to-the-holy-pascha-week.pdf [Accessed 09 April 2021].

H.G, Anba Serapion, 2004. Treasures of the Fathers of the Church Volume Three. 1st ed. Diocese of Los Angeles: St Paul Brotherhood.

Mikhail, Deacon Albair Gamal, *The Essentials in the Deacon's Service,* (Shobra, Egypt: Shikolani, 2002), Translated from Arabic by Mina Barsoum, edited by Alexander A-Malek and Ragy Sharkawy.

PNGKey. [online] Available at: https://www.pngkey.com/ [Accessed 14 April 2021].

Shutterstock. [online] Available at: https://www.shutterstock.com/ [Accessed 14 April 2021].

Tasbeha.org: Coptic Hymns, Praises, and Divine Liturgies. 2013. Tasbeha.org: Coptic Hymns, Praises, and Divine Liturgies. [online] Available at: http://www.tasbeha.org. [Accessed 10 April 2021].

Twinkl. [online] Available at: https://www.twinkl.com.au/ [Accessed 17 March 2021].

Vecteezy. [online] Available at: https://www.vecteezy.com [Accessed 17 March 2021].

St. John the Evangelist and St. Verena Coptic Orthodox Church

583 Orrong Road, Armadale, Vic 3143, Australia

For any inquires please visit the Church Website
www.stverenaschurch.org
or email: stjohntheevangelistmedia@gmail.com

Made in United States
North Haven, CT
22 April 2022

18491118R00044